Original title:
A Brooch for All Seasons

Copyright © 2025 Creative Arts Management OÜ
All rights reserved.

Author: Cameron Blair
ISBN HARDBACK: 978-1-80586-184-3
ISBN PAPERBACK: 978-1-80586-656-5

Mesmerizing Through the Months

In January's chill, I don a pin,
Shaped like a snowman, with a goofy grin.
He wobbles on my scarf, what a sight!
Each gust of wind gives him such a fright!

As spring arrives, I swap him for a bee,
Buzzing cheerfully, all happy and free.
Flower power pinned right on my chest,
My buzzing buddy puts my style to the test!

When summer hits, it's a sun in my hair,
Glowing brightly without a single care.
Dance in the sun, oh, what a delight,
This shining treasure makes everything bright!

Autumn's here, I grab a leafy clip,
Dancing with colors, watch my style flip.
With each falling leaf my brooch starts to sway,
Laughing together, in a joyful array!

So through each month, my pin takes a stand,
A funny companion, always close at hand.
From snowmen to sun, in nature's grand play,
Fashion and laughter make up my bouquet!

The Timeless Fasteners

In springtime, bright with flowers' cheer,
A clasp of daisies struts so near.
While summer sunbeams warm the air,
A flamingo pin shows off with flair.

When autumn leaves begin to fall,
A pumpkin patch adorns the hall.
In winter's chill, a snowman glows,
Ensuring warmth, where laughter flows.

Glimmers Through the Year

A unicorn against the blue,
Blinks back with dreams of candy chew.
In February, hearts beat fast,
With Valentine's bling, love unsurpassed.

A turkey at Thanksgiving's feast,
Winks with a smile, not meant to tease.
By Christmas, elves in sparkly ties,
Dance upon the tree, oh my, oh my!

Whispered Memories in Metal

Once wore a pin of grandma's cat,
Now it's my turn to wear that brat!
With every season, a tale unfolds,
Of past and present, of friendships bold.

An owl for wisdom, so they say,
Winks at the mishaps of our day.
Through laughter, tears, and playful jest,
These trinkets hold our memories best.

A Heirloom's Embrace

Granddad's tie pin, a dapper style,
Keeps me grinning all the while.
In summer heat, with shorts I wear,
His fashion tips, beyond compare.

A butterfly from sister dear,
Flutters around, ignites good cheer.
As seasons change, our laughter stays,
In every clasp, joy always plays.

Enchantment in Every Twist.

A sparkling gem caught in a twist,
Shiny and bright, it can't be missed.
My cat thinks it's a tasty snack,
When I turn away, it's gone, oh, the lack!

Around my neck, it wanders free,
A dance of colors, what could it be?
A squirrel stopped by to give it a spin,
Now I have a furry friend, let the chaos begin!

Gems of Every Dawn

Each morning brings a gem anew,
Yesterday's charm just won't do.
But I left it out near my tea,
Now the dog wears it, look at him flee!

With every sunrise, a gleam and a laugh,
They sparkle and shine, each a silly gaffe.
I tried to wear one, but it flew to a bee,
Who buzzed in delight, oh let it be free!

Seasons Adorned in Elegance

Winter's trinkets—snowflakes and frost,
But I dropped mine, now it's completely lost.
Spring brings flowers, lovely and bright,
But my brooch now thinks it's ready for flight!

Summer shines with a colorful flair,
Each piece a story, beyond compare.
But I tripped on my daisies, oh what a sight,
Now it's a necklace for a passing kite!

The Timeless Adornment

This timeless piece, so full of glee,
Wants to be more than it can be.
I tried to fix it, but it ran away,
Sporting a bandit mask, what a display!

Adorning my hat, it took to the sky,
I waved my goodbye, it gave a sly sigh.
Oh, what a journey, from brooch to a dream,
In a world of fancy, it reigns supreme!

The Art of Transformation

A pin that dances, what a sight,
Transforms a flop, makes day seem bright.
Turning shirts to fancy wear,
With just a twist, it's style and flair.

From drab to fab, it's quite a feat,
A funny fix for those in heat.
It sparkles, shines in feline grace,
Add some bling, it's a whole new face.

Crafted for Every Horizon

A gem for every season's play,
Turns a frown into a bouquet.
From summer sun to winter's chill,
A cheeky wink, it bends to will.

Worn with joy, or sometimes jest,
It knows how to keep you dressed best.
A little croak, a frog, a bee,
Each day it whispers, "Look at me!"

Nature's Embrace in Metal

A leaf-shaped trinket, grasp it tight,
It's nature's giggle, pure delight.
From falls to blooms, it loves to sway,
In morning light, it steals the day.

An acorn, a flower, all in one,
It makes you laugh, it's so much fun.
In sun or rain, it finds its charm,
With every clip, it means no harm.

The Language of Luster

With shiny words, it speaks so loud,
Each glint and gleam, it feels so proud.
Quirky tales in colors bold,
It's more than metal, it's worth its gold.

A rainbow twist that twirls with glee,
Sparks conversations, as you can see.
In laughter's pulse, it finds its muse,
An artful jest, it'll never lose.

Charms of Life's Tapestry

A pin of laughter, bright and bold,
Worn as a story, a joy to behold.
It jingles and jangles, a quirky hue,
A tale of the day when fashion was new.

In pockets it hides, from the rain and the sun,
A sassy companion, a little bit fun.
Threaded in moments, forever entwined,
A chuckle in metal, a treasure to find.

A Dance of Colors and Light

With polka dots dancing, twirling about,
The colors collide, without any doubt.
A wink from the sun, a glow from the moon,
They shimmy together, a vibrant cartoon.

In spring it's a daisy, in winter it's snow,
Each season's a party, just watch the show!
Giggles erupt with each sunny turn,
In the spotlight of life, it's your turn to burn.

Nature's Cherished Keepsake

A leaf and a pebble, a seed and a stone,
Each one a memory, each one a throne.
Found in a garden or on a walk,
They're cheeky reminders, just start the talk!

The ocean's small treasures, all shiny and neat,
Compose a collection that's hard to beat.
Each season collects with a wink and a cheer,
Nature's keepsakes, forever sincere.

Reflections of the Earth

A mirror of giggles, a splash of delight,
The world wears its charm, so shiny and bright.
With every bead twinkling in place,
It's a riddle of moments, each holding a face.

As clouds drift like feathers, all fluffy and light,
The earth hums a tune that feels just right.
A whimsical journey, the dance never ends,
In laughter and light, where the world always bends.

Gems of Every Shade

In springtime's bloom, a red delight,
A sparkly cherry, oh what a sight!
Summer brings yellow, bright as the sun,
A playful lemon, just for fun.

Autumn's gold, it twinkles with glee,
A brave little pumpkin, can't you see?
Winter's icy, a frosty blue,
A cheeky snowflake, just for you!

Adornments of Time

Tick-tock goes the watch, oh what a tease!
A winking owl, just doing as it please.
Seconds slip by with a wink and a nod,
While it giggles softly, quick as a god.

Calendar smiles, adorned with a bow,
A wacky anchor, where shall we go?
Each month it winks, then struts in line,
Dancing through time, oh so divine!

The Enchanted Pin

A pin of magic, once found in a straw,
With sparkles and giggles that drop jaws.
It sits on my coat, showing off its flair,
Making every dull day, a fun affair.

It flutters like birds, it ticks like a clock,
A whimsical friend, a party in stock!
Jokes hidden inside, oh boy what a thrill,
For laughter is gold, and it fits like a chill.

Everlasting Elegance

In the corner sits a pin, aloof and grand,
With a wink in its shine - it's got the upper hand.
It teases the other jewels, so proud and slick,
Saying, 'I'm the star, this isn't just a trick!'

It dresses up shirts, adds sass to a hat,
Grinning at dresses, 'You think that is that?'
A dance in the light, a jester's embrace,
Everlasting elegance, gone without a trace!

An Emblem of Change

Once a butterfly, now a snail,
With each pinning, a new tale.
Worn with pride or worn with shame,
Fashion's just a silly game.

Sunshine today, tomorrow rain,
On my jacket, a dancing brain.
Mood swings pinned in bright array,
Fashion fumbles, come what may.

Echoes in Enamel

Glistening greens, electric blues,
Guess my brooch? Oh, what's your views?
An owl, a cat, or maybe cheese,
Worn with laughter, fashion's tease.

Every snapshot, an art escape,
Matching with my overly large cape.
When in doubt, just wear a grin,
Best accessory? The chaos within.

Beauty that Transcends

A flamingo on a rainy day,
Wobbling pins in a glorious sway.
My grandma's treasure, not for sale,
She said style's but a silly tale.

In the office, on a date,
What's that shimmer? Oh, it's fate!
Dressed to impress, or just for fun,
A fashion disaster, she's number one!

Gems in the Garden

In my garden, a sparkly bee,
Sharing laughter with a wobbly tree.
A flower here, a vase misplaced,
Nature's chaos, so closely traced.

Twirling daisies, blooming bold,
Adventures in fashion, stories retold.
With each season, something new to glean,
The garden's humor is often unseen.

Threads of Diversity

In spring, she dons a daisy pin,
A bounce of joy, a cheeky grin.
Summer brings a sun so bright,
With shades of yellow, pure delight.

Autumn's hues, a pumpkin charm,
Keep it close, it brings such calm.
Winter wraps around in snow,
With frosty gems that steal the show.

The Essence of Every Season

Spring showers bring a raindrop flair,
A curl of silver meets the air.
Summer sizzles with beachy bliss,
A cocktail clasp sealed with a kiss.

Fall's colors dance, a rustling cheer,
A leaf-shaped piece that's quite sincere.
Winter sparkles with icy cheer,
Glittering lights, the end is near.

Captured Moments in Grace

A summer breeze, a seashell sways,
It tickles the sun in sunny days.
Autumn whispers, a scarf in tow,
With leaf-shaped gems that steal the show.

Winter's chill with a penguin flair,
A snowy cap sits on the wearer's hair.
Springtime blooms bring playful tones,
A floral pin that steals our phones.

Jewels of the Year

From frosty nights with shiny pins,
To sunny days where laughter spins.
Each season's charm, a quirky twist,
In every look, you must persist.

A glitter here, a sparkle there,
Collect them all, if you dare!
For fun awaits in every hue,
Wear them proudly, tried and true!

Flourishes from Frost to Bloom

In winter's chill, I wear a pin,
To spark a laugh, let fun begin.
A snowman's hat, a jolly sight,
Makes frosty days feel oh-so-bright.

Come springtime blooms, I change my tune,
A butterfly to dance in June.
It tickles folks, a light affair,
With nature's flair, I've got to share.

In summer's sun, a radiant spark,
A flamingo struts, it hits the mark.
With shades and laughs all intertwined,
My style's a giggle, well-defined.

When autumn calls, I take the chance,
A pumpkin brooch makes everyone prance.
A harvest theme, let's celebrate,
With laughter in this special fate.

Allure in Every Phase

From winter's frost, I wear a pine,
A quirky charm that's still divine.
It cracks a smile, a playful jest,
In snowflakes' dance, I feel the zest.

As sunbeams break, I hop and sway,
A daisy pin brightens up the day.
With giggles shared among my friends,
This charm of mine just never ends.

In summer's fun, a silly fish,
Winks and wiggles, fulfilling a wish.
With laughter loud beneath the sun,
In every phase, we share the fun.

When autumn comes, I'll let it show,
A squirrel's grin as leaves do blow.
With whimsy wrapped in every glance,
In every brooch, we find our chance.

Evolving Elegance

In frosty days, a quirky fox,
Perched upon my coat, it rocks!
With fluffy tails, it prances free,
Bringing smiles to you and me.

As tulips bloom, I switch it up,
A ladybug upon my cup.
It rolls around, a playful tease,
With laughter shared upon the breeze.

In sizzling heat, a sunlit bee,
Dances in glee, just wait and see.
Buzzing about, it brings delight,
A golden laugh in warm daylight.

When leaves turn gold, I wear a bat,
Halloween charm, imagine that!
With giggles shared 'neath starlit skies,
In shifting styles, fun never dies.

Together Through Time's Tides

In winter's hold, a snow globe spins,
Inside a laugh where cold begins.
With frosty whimsy, we all play,
And joke about the snowy fray.

When spring arrives, a flower blooms,
A comical hat that chases glooms.
With petals bright and smiles wide,
In every stitch, the fun won't hide.

Under the sun, a jolly sun,
A playful grin, let's have some fun!
With lemonade and laughs so sweet,
As summer's warmth kicks to the beat.

In autumn's glow, a cheeky ghost,
Scares up giggles, that's the most!
With jokes and spooks, we dance around,
Through seasons' change, our joy is found.

Whispered Jewels of Nature

Tiny acorns, quite the thrill,
Dancing on branches, oh what a chill!
Squirrels in tuxedos, oh so spry,
Nature's bling sparkling in the sky.

Crickets chirp in silver attire,
As the sun sets, they never tire.
A glowworm's party under a leaf,
Fashion in shadows, beyond belief!

Frogs in sequins, ready to croak,
They'll ribbit you silly with their joke.
With every leap, a new style's born,
Fashionably late, in the misty dawn.

A pumpkin's smile, oh what a jest,
In autumn charm, it's dressed the best.
With vines as accessories, growing bold,
Nature's runway, stories untold.

Radiance through the Year

Winter's frost in diamond dust,
Snowflakes twirl, oh how they gust!
Hot cocoa mugs with marshmallow hats,
Winter wears bling, and that's a fact!

Springtime blooms in colors so bright,
Bumblebees buzzing, taking flight.
Tulips in slippers, pink and yellow,
Nature's party, come on, say hello!

Summer sun in shades of gold,
Flip-flops clack, oh so bold!
Beach balls bounce in joyous cheer,
A tan so glamorous, let's all revere!

Autumn leaves, the grand finale,
Parading in colors, oh so jolly.
Pumpkins pose in a patch parade,
A season of laughter, never a fade.

Petals and Pearls

Petals abound, a floral spree,
Tiny ladybugs sip on tea.
Daisy chains sparkle like crown jewels,
Nature's odd fashion show in cools.

Butterflies flaunt their fabric flair,
Sipping nectar with a stylish air.
Each bloom's a story, a raucous laugh,
Nature's runway, an endless gaffe!

Rustling leaves in their wind-swept dance,
A spiral twirl as nature prance.
Winking daisies, how they tease,
Fashion critters in the summer breeze.

Goldfinches wear their feathered best,
Gathering joy in nature's fest.
Come join the fun, on this grand stage,
Petals and pearls, all take the page!

Verses of Versatility

A sunflower hat? Now that's a sight,
Swaying in the field, feeling just right.
Lemonade lakes with ice cube flair,
Refreshing gigs, everywhere!

The wind tosses curls, a wild caress,
Kites in the sky, a colorful mess.
Rainbow choices, they flip and float,
Life's a giggle, keep the good note!

Fluffy clouds as cotton candy,
Whispers of giggles, oh so dandy.
Rain boots splashing, puddles galore,
Who knew fun could come from the floor?

Feathers and sparkles, all intertwined,
This vibrant tapestry, each thread aligned.
In every season, quirkiness thrives,
Fashion's a laugh, where humor derives!

Enchantment in Every Event

At a wedding, I wore a pin,
Shaped like a fish, oh what a win!
Caught the eye of Auntie Sue,
She laughed so hard, her drink just flew.

A birthday bash, all balloons and cheer,
My sparkly star made quite a smear.
"Is that a trophy?" someone pondered,
I grinned and said, "It's my honor!"

At the office, I sported a flair,
A tiny cactus with a spiky hair.
My coworkers raised an eyebrow high,
"Is that plant alive? Does it even try?"

Seasons change, but laughs remain,
With quirky pins, I'll entertain!
From snowflakes crisp to summer suns,
My jeweled jest leaves all in runs.

Hues of Harmony

In spring, I wore a flower bright,
Its petals flopped, what a sight!
Everyone said, "That's quite a bloom,"
I laughed and twirled, gave it some zoom.

Summer came with sunshine bold,
I sported a sun with rays of gold.
Kids asked if I'd melt in heat,
I winked and danced, light on my feet.

Autumn hues called for leaves in red,
My brooch curled up like a cozy bed.
"Why not wear a pumpkin instead?"
I just smiled, "This leaf is my thread!"

Then winter's chill brought snowflakes fine,
Wore one that sparkled, it felt divine.
Neighbors gasped, "Is that legit?"
I chuckled, "Sure, if it fits!"

An Ode to Nature's Grace

In the garden, a bee took flight,
I had a pin that buzzed with delight.
With wings so bright and a smile so wide,
It seemed to dance with nature's pride.

At picnics, I wore a butterfly,
It fluttered out, I couldn't deny.
Friends claimed it might just take off,
I told them, "Don't scoff, it's just soft!"

When winter came with snow on the spruce,
I found a penguin, oh what a truce!
"Is your bird cold?" my friend did ask,
I said, "Nope, it's got a winter task!"

Nature's gems, they stir no stress,
Each cheeky piece, I wear with finesse.
From floral dreams to beasts of cheer,
In every season, joy appears near.

Lattice of Life

Woke up one day feeling quite bold,
Adorned with a spider that sparkled gold.
My friends were worried I'd lose my way,
"Don't you think it might pray?"

To the party, I brought a cheese Swiss,
A wheel with holes—oh, what a bliss!
"Is it snacktime?" someone inquired,
"Oh no, it's fashion," I simply fired.

Autumn leaves wrapped on my coat,
Wore a squirrel who thought it could float.
"Does that furry fella hold your snacks?"
"Only acorns," I gave some cracks!

And winter's chill brought a frosty frost,
A snowman brooch that looked quite lost.
"Did you buy that on a whim?" they teased,
I chuckled, "Only when I'm pleased!"

Ephemeral Elegance

A shiny pin that gleams so bright,
It dances on my coat of white.
A butterfly with glasses shades,
It flutters where the laughter trades.

In spring it wears a bloom so bold,
In winter, snowflakes made of gold.
Each season's jest, a playful tease,
A clamp on joy, just like a breeze.

Nature's Woven Whimsy

A leaf that curls, oh what a sight,
It whispers secrets day and night.
With threads of grass and petals fine,
It chuckles softly, "A toast to wine!"

In summer sun, it might just tan,
In autumn's chill, it shifts its plan.
An acorn cap—such chic attire,
Dancing through leaves, a woodsy choir.

A Spectrum of Sentiments

A pin of change, it grins and sways,
From glowing red to sunny rays.
A frown that flips, a laugh, a pout,
It's fashion's game—what's that about?

In moods it shifts like clouds above,
From stormy grey to hearts of love.
A polka dot or stripes of glee,
Each color tells a tale for free.

Treasures of the Evergreen

A pinecone shard on my lapel,
It jingles softly, tells a tale.
With needles tucked and berries bright,
It teases squirrels from morning light.

In winter's breath, it wears some frost,
In summer's warmth, it finds what's lost.
A charm that grows with every scene,
In nature's arms, forever keen.

Embers of Seasons Past

In winter's chill, I find a pin,
It sparkles bright, like frosty skin.
Spring blooms forth, in colors bold,
I clip it on, my style retold.

When summer heat turns up the fun,
A flowered gem catches the sun.
Fall's leaves dance in a golden swirl,
I sport my brooch, oh what a twirl!

Each season brings a laugh or two,
A quirky charm, what can I do?
With every pin, a silly tale,
Of sun and snow, of wind and sail.

So here I go, my laughter glows,
With every chapter that I chose.
Each brooch I wear, a whimsy cast,
In memories bright, and love amassed!

Jewels of the Earth

A pebble brooch from yesterday,
It fell where I took time to play.
In muddy shoes, my fashion blooms,
My friends all laugh, in silly rooms.

A stick and stone ensemble shines,
With nature's flair, my heart aligns.
The dirt, the grass, my frolicking style,
Nature's gift, it makes me smile!

Oh, quartz and clay, what joy you bring,
In campfire glow, we laugh and sing.
My treasures found, in every nook,
With rocks and gems, we'll write a book!

As seasons turn and laughter swells,
Adorned in earth's own tale it tells.
With every piece, a funny spree,
I wear my treasures joyfully!

The Stories We Wear

I found a tale upon my chest,
A button brooch that I love best.
Each color speaks of days gone past,
Where silly moments forever last.

From napping cats to dancing socks,
My badges show my quirky flocks.
A conversation starter, too,
With friends who smile at what I do.

Each piece I choose, a laugh to spark,
A tale of joy that leaves a mark.
The stories told, they never cease,
In laughter's glow, I find my peace.

As whispers weave in every seam,
My wardrobe sings, it's like a dream.
With every charm, a witful cheer,
The stories worn, forever near!

Nature's Artistry Unbound

In gardens bright, my pins do sprout,
Each petal shines, there's no doubt.
With laughter's hue and playful flair,
I wear the earth, without a care!

A ladybug, oh what a sight,
It winks at me both day and night.
The butterfly flits cheerfully,
In nature's art, we're wild and free!

With daisies, roses, thorns, and all,
My wardrobe's turned into a ball.
Each flower tells a funny tale,
Of bee hugs, rains, and windy gales.

So here I flaunt my crafty finds,
With nature's love, no ties that bind.
In every piece, a chuckle found,
In life's grand dance, we're spellbound!

Eternal Tokens of Time

In summer's sun, a sparkly pin,
It holds my shirt when my waistline's thin.
A winter jewel, with flakes of ice,
But loses charm when my cat thinks it's nice.

Autumn leaves caught in a silver clasp,
I wore it once, then found it—oops—gasp!
Spring buds bloomed on my collar's edge,
Now they just hang—what a strange pledge!

A timepiece stuck in a fashion craze,
It tells the time in the funniest ways.
With a wink and a nudge, it makes me grin,
Who knew fashion could be such a win!

This trinket spins tales of laughter and cheer,
Each season's folly is vividly clear.
With laughter on tow, I gleefully see,
These tokens of time are just meant for me.

Fragments of Frost and Flame

A blazing sunbeam in my lapel,
Yet it melts away when I trip and fell.
A frosty gem from a winter's plot,
That sparkles and shines but it's easily caught.

In springtime's breeze, a flower spins,
But so do my worries when the pollen begins.
Summer's heat turns my pin into goo,
My outfit's a mess, but hey, it's quite new!

With autumn hues, my chest's finely dressed,
Yet leaves join in, they think they're impressed.
They twist and turn, and I can't keep track,
Seasons collide, and garments just lack.

Frost bites and flames in this fashion show,
Each part of me blinks with a striking glow.
These fragments of crises make me feel gleeful,
Who knew a pin could be so deceitful!

Seasons in a Stone

A tiny gem in my fall sweater,
It warms my heart but I swear it's better.
Spring's sparkle brings joy at every glance,
Yet everyone stared when I tried to dance.

Summer's heat turned my brooch to glue,
I'm fashionably stuck, oh what can I do?
As winter comes, it freezes tight,
It's a chilly affair—that's quite a fright!

As seasons twirl in their colorful glee,
My stone takes the stage, oh what a spree!
Fragments of laughter, with joy I compose,
But watch out for cats—they'll steal it, who knows?

Through seasons entwined, I chuckle and sigh,
This shiny stone makes my spirits fly.
Who would've thought such a gem is a jokester?
Each twist and turn, a whimsical toaster!

The Jewelry of Moments

A trinket of laughter, I wore it with pride,
In moments of chaos, it sparkles and snide.
A burst of humor in dull, dreary days,
Wrapped snug in my vest, it continues to play.

With moments of laughter in every nook,
It winks at the world, like a sneaky old crook.
From birthdays to bumbles, this jewel's got flair,
It sparkles with mischief, a bonafide dare!

In summer's hot days, it melts in the heat,
Yet turns up the fun with its mischievous beat.
When autumn winds howl, it shivers with glee,
Each moment it captures, so silly and free.

Through the seasons it dances, my jewelry bold,
In stories of laughter, its tale will unfold.
This charm of a trinket, so bright, and so true,
Makes every dull moment a vibrant debut!

Seasons Worn in Style

In springtime's bloom, the daisies play,
A pop of color, in a quirky way.
With butterflies that tease and flit,
They pin on joy, just a little bit.

Summer sizzles, the sun does shine,
I wear a flip-flop, so divine.
A cocktail glass, sure looks just right,
Sparkling laughter, day turns to night.

Autumn's chill gives way to cheer,
With acorns stored, oh dear, oh dear!
A pin of orange, red leaves abound,
Who knew fashion could spin round?

Winter brings a frosty breeze,
Wrapped in sweaters, oh, such ease!
A snowman brooch atop my chest,
Fashion's fun, it's truly best!

Threads of Nature's Grace

Each season spins a tale of flair,
Worn on coats, with dazzling care.
From vibrant spring, to winter's chill,
Nature's humor gives us a thrill.

A leaf that's pinned, or an ice cream cone,
Fashion evolves, but we're never alone.
A winking sun, with a wink it beams,
We strut our stuff, in laughter it seems.

Summer's bright hues, like a fruit bazaar,
A watermelon slice, it's seen from afar.
With sunglasses perched, and a grin so wide,
Clothing tells tales, let style be our guide.

When leaves turn gold, I must confess,
A pumpkin charm brings me happiness.
Who knew a little flair could tease?
Life's a runway, with such ease!

A Dance of Colors

In spring's embrace, we twirl and spin,
With pastel petals, let the fun begin.
A daffodil brooch, gives a fluffy nod,
Who wears it better? Not a single flawed.

Summer's heat, we dance about,
With bright tropics, there's no doubt.
A sun with shades, and a cheeky smile,
We strut in style, walk that extra mile.

Fall shows off its fiery dress,
A scarecrow pin, oh what a mess!
With leaves to crunch beneath our toes,
We march with laughter, as the cool wind blows.

Winter wraps us, snug and tight,
With snowflakes dripping, a dazzling sight.
A penguin pin with a jolly sway,
We slide through the season, hip-hip-hooray!

Emblems of Change

The sun arrives with a cheery grin,
Floral prints, let the fun begin!
A bee that's buzzing, or a bloom that's bright,
Fashion's a game, a delightful sight.

When summers hot, we mix and match,
Wearing the world like a fashion patch.
A beach ball pin, and a sun-kissed gold,
In this crazy dance, let stories unfold!

As leaves turn crisp, let's gather round,
A cozy charm, with warmth profound.
Pumpkin smiles and the crunch of frost,
Emblems of change, we're never lost.

In winter's chill, I wear my snow,
A frosty gem, with a twinkling glow.
With warmth from laughter that we create,
Style is timeless; come celebrate!

A Continuum of Beauty

In summer's sun, it shines so bright,
A winking, blinking, flashy sight.
Winter comes, and it won't hide,
With frosty flair, it wears with pride.

Spring arrives with blooms so grand,
It dances lightly, hand in hand.
Fall's leaves crunch beneath its gleam,
A playful twist, a fashion dream.

The Charm of Hues

It wears every color, what a treat,
Red for the bold, blue's quite neat.
Yellow's laughter, green's surprise,
Purple's charm that never lies.

Spinning round, it takes the stage,
A seasonal jest, it's all the rage.
Festive sparkle, day or night,
It's always ready for delight!

Timelessness Embodied

A sprightly flicker in a timeless dance,
With every outfit, it'll take a chance.
In moments grand, or days so bland,
It makes a scene, quite unplanned.

From silly parties to formal cheer,
It knows no bounds, it has no fear.
With playful twists, it finds a way,
To brighten up the dullest day.

Seasons of Sparkle

In winter's chill, it twinkles bright,
A diamond dazzle, pure delight.
Summer's warmth brings all the flair,
It sparkles while we breathe the air.

Leaves may fall, yet it stands tall,
With every glance, the heart will call.
Through snowy nights to sunny rays,
It's a gem that dances in many ways.

Nature's Gift of Adornment

In springtime blooms with colors bright,
A dandelion on my shirt, what a sight!
Bees buzz around, trying to claim,
My new fashion choice, oh what a game!

Summer's sun, a quirky hat,
With flowers glued, my head looks like that!
Birds laugh as they fly on by,
"Is that a garden?" they seem to cry!

Autumn leaves, a playful scene,
Stuck to my coat, they look quite keen.
I'm the walking forest, can you tell?
Nature's gifts, they suit me well!

Winter's frost, I sport a pine,
Sprouting branches, looking divine!
Snowflakes dance, their beauty to share,
Wearing my tree, I'm debonair!

Whispers of Wisdom

Grandma says, 'Adorn with care,'
'A sock on your hat's quite rare!'
I nod along, with a wink for fun,
Fashion advice, I won't shun!

Uncles wear ties with silly themes,
Fish and hats, or so it seems!
Funny socks and mismatched shoes,
Every holiday, wear the blues!

A brooch of buttons from the past,
On my jacket, it's quite a blast!
Each piece tells a fun-filled tale,
With every laugh, I'll surely prevail!

So gather round, let's dress absurd,
And let the world hear each wise word.
With outfits bold and laughter loud,
In style's embrace, we feel so proud!

A Tapestry of Time

In days of yore, with styles so grand,
A pocket watch can barely stand!
With wild hair and polka dots,
History laughs, oh, how it trots!

Medieval knights wore armor bright,
But checkered pants? Oh what a sight!
While dragons lurked, they'd strut and sway,
In their finest garb, come what may!

Renaissance days, a ruffled collar,
With colors that just seem to holler!
But pickles stuck on it for flair,
It surely made the fashion rare!

Fast forward now, to selfie scenes,
With filters, fun, and quirky themes.
Each snap shows us in bold delight,
Wearing our laughs with all our might!

Treasury of Temperaments

With moods that flutter like a kite,
One day I'm sunny, the next I bite!
A smiley face cape for joyful gleam,
And frowny socks when I'm not in theme!

Comfy and cozy, I call it a win,
Pajamas all day—let's begin!
Mix and match, who needs a rhyme?
Fashion is wild, and so is my time!

With rainclouds looming, I'll wear a grin,
A hat like a mushroom, where do I begin?
Every piece shows how I feel,
Fashionable fun is the real deal!

So let's embrace every quirky dress,
Wearing our hearts, we always impress.
From goofy hats to mismatched shoes,
In this treasure, we simply can't lose!

An Array of Allure

In spring, I wear a daffodil,
With petals bright and cheer,
It pins me down to smiles and thrills,
And chases away all fear.

In summer, I don sunglasses,
A brooch that shines so bright,
It blinds the sun and also classes,
A fashionista's delight.

In autumn, leaves begin to fall,
I sport acorns for the fun,
They clink and clatter, what a ball,
Creating laughs, not just for one.

In winter, icy sparkles dance,
A snowflake on my chest,
It sparkles with a frosty glance,
With this accessory, I'm the best!

Seasons Entwined

In spring, my brooch is full of blooms,
A garden pinned right on my shirt,
I swear it shouts, 'No more dull rooms!'
While saying, 'Watch out for the dirt!'

Summer shines with jelly beans,
A sugary burst of color bright,
I wear them proudly, oh what scenes!
A snack and style that feels just right.

When fall arrives with crunchy leaves,
A tiny pumpkin joins the throng,
Each sway and wiggle, goodness! It grieves,
When I forget to sing the song!

And winter brings the culprit—snow,
A fancier than Frosty's hat,
My chilly charm steals all the show,
With laughter loud, it's such a spat!

A Celebration of Change

Springtime bunnies hop and sway,
On my collar, oh, what glee!
They wink and wiggle all the way,
And keep my spirits wild and free.

Summer comes with seashell bling,
I anchor fun with ocean hues,
Each shell a funky little fling,
Sounding like the best of blues.

As fall arrives, they turn to spice,
I pin on pumpkins, oh soround!
Their giggles could suffice,
To cover up my clueless frown.

Then winter's chill brings crafty cheer,
A brooch that jingles—what a sound!
With every clink, I spread the cheer,
Warming hearts as seasons round!

The Jewel of Experience

Spring hops forth with vibrant hues,
A ladybug stuck on my coat,
It zooms and zips, oh what a muse,
It's laughter's secret antidote!

In summer's heat, a sun is found,
Stuck to my lapel with flair,
Sweating cricket sounds all around,
Fashion genius? Why, that's rare!

Autumn's charm brings chestnuts bright,
I twirl in style with crunchy joy,
Each nut a burst of fun, delight,
While teasing squirrels—oh, what a ploy!

Winter lands with icy stares,
A snowman brooch holds frosty jive,
With every chill, it loudly declares,
"Who needs a coat? I'm still alive!"

Transformations in Brocade

In summer's sun, a flower blooms,
A brocade cat turns, chasing grooms.
In winter's chill, it dons a scarf,
Playing dress-up, it loves to laugh.

In autumn's hues, it wears a crown,
A leafy wonder, never a frown.
Spring brings colors, bright and fair,
Dancing around like it doesn't care.

With each twist, it finds a smile,
A party piece for every style.
From plaid to polka, it won't be beat,
Transformations that are oh-so sweet.

So wear it bright, or wear it plain,
This timeless gem, a fashion chain.
With charm and wit, it makes you muse,
A playful spirit you can't refuse.

The Kaleidoscope Keeper

A sparkly gem, a tale unfolds,
In every shift, it brightly molds.
With every glance, a giggle grows,
A silly wink where fashion flows.

From daisies to stripes, it takes a leap,
A colorful swirl, not one to keep.
With shades that change and faces too,
This playful piece makes old seem new.

In every season, it plays a role,
A jester's heart, it's on a roll.
From blue to pink, it loves the prank,
On every outfit, it leaves a thank.

Through laughter's lens and joy's embrace,
This keeper shines, a lively grace.
In every heart, it plants a jest,
Wearing a smile, it's simply the best.

Seasons Adorned

Springtime flings with blossoms bright,
This gem delights, a silly sight.
In summer's heat, it wears a hat,
Sun-kissed laughter, oh, imagine that!

When autumn comes, it hugs a leaf,
With quirky charm, it brings relief.
In winter's frost, it wears some snow,
Joking with snowmen, putting on a show.

Each season whispers, "Come and play!",
With colors popping night and day.
It flips and flops like a dancing fish,
In fashion's pond, it grants a wish.

So wear it proud, let laughter ring,
This piece of fun makes spirits sing.
With every season, it breaks the norm,
A joyful dance in a playful form.

Echoes of Fashion's Flow

Echoes ring from every thread,
A comical twist, where laughs are fed.
With every style, a joke unfolds,
This charming piece never grows old.

From ruffled edges to sequined bliss,
It catches winks, and it begs a kiss.
In crowded rooms, it steals the scene,
A fashionista, so bright and green.

With giggles sewn in every seam,
This joyous gem is quite the dream.
From silly bows to twinkling stars,
It laughs aloud in fancy bars.

So pin it on and let it shine,
With happy hearts, all things align.
In every laugh, our styles will meet,
An echoing joy that's ever sweet.

The Light of Seasons

Spring brings flowers, bright and bold,
A pin of petals, stories told.
Summer shines with sunbeam flair,
A splash of color everywhere.

Autumn leaves, a swirling dance,
Worn as a pendant, a silly chance.
Winter's chill, a frosty note,
Pinned on a scarf or a warm coat.

Each season's change, a playful twist,
Accessorize with a cheeky fist.
With every month, a brand new style,
A giggle here, a wink, a smile.

So wear your trinkets, laugh and cheer,
For every season brings good cheer.
A laughter stitch to hold so dear,
In shiny metal, love sincere.

Elegance in Every Epoch

In days of yore, a lady's grace,
A fancy pin, a charming face.
With lace and ruffles, frills galore,
She'd wear her gems and then explore.

Victorian cuffs, they turn and swirl,
A glimmering jewel to catch a whirl.
Jazz-age parties, a sparkly brooch,
Twist and twirl, let's go encroach!

Modern times, a quirky flair,
Feathers and charms, fun everywhere.
From retro days to future's sight,
Each little piece just feels so right.

So dance through time with joy unbound,
In every epoch, laughter found.
For elegance can surely roam,
In vintage style, we find our home.

Glinting Through Generations

Grandma's clasp, a shining gem,
It holds the tales of our dear kin.
With stories spun, and laughter's thread,
Legacy pinned, we laugh instead.

Mom wore it bright at her first dance,
A shimmering heart, a daring romance.
Yesterday's treasures, today's delight,
Sprinkling joy in the moonlit night.

Children giggle, swap and trade,
A picnic party, making a parade.
For each sweet memory, a shiny brooch,
A sparkly keeper, no need to reproach.

From hand to hand, the shine will last,
Seasons may change, but fun's a blast.
Together we gleam through every age,
In glinting trinkets, we turn the page.

A Kaleidoscope of Charm

A daisy pin, all bright and twirling,
A swirl of colors, joy unfurling.
With polka dots and funky shapes,
Worn on a hat, oh, what escapes!

Neon hues, let's make a scene,
With sparkly dazzles, we're like a dream.
Layer those brooches, more the fun,
It's a playful style for everyone!

Aging gracefully, a silver snitch,
Adds a cheeky charm, oh what a pitch!
From winks and giggles to blushing flair,
A jeweled laugh, light as air.

So mix it up, let colors clash,
With all this sparkle, let's start a bash!
For in this dance of style and cheer,
Kaleidoscopes twinkle, crystal clear.

Guardian of Femininity

In a garden of colors, I pin with glee,
A cat on my lap, it's a sight to see.
With every occasion, a sparkly switch,
I strut like a peacock, a fabulous glitch.

My friends all request, 'Lend us your flair!',
'The glittery magic that you love to wear.'
I wink and I nod, like a fairy in flight,
'Tis the charms of my treasures that bring pure delight!

Old jeans and a sweater, but wait—what's that?
A butterfly treasure, now look at me strut!
The drab turns to fab with a flick of my wrist,
In the world of chic, you just can't resist.

So here's to the sparkle that brightens my days,
With laughter and joy in oh-so-many ways!
Every little trinket tells stories anew,
In the game of glam, it's a fun rendezvous.

The Shimmering Tapestry

A tapestry woven with laughter and love,
Each piece a story, a treasure trove.
With colors that dance and fabrics that gleam,
I wear my joy like a vibrant dream.

My quirky collection, oh what a sight,
Feathers and sparkles that twinkle at night.
I sport a fine penguin with a mischievous grin,
Who knew such odd things could make me win?

Each gathering calls for my best-dressed charade,
A wild, silly charm parade, unafraid.
My friends all gather, their laughter resounds,
Who knew accessories could turn life around?

So here's to the shimmer in joyful display,
Let's giggle and sparkle, come join the fray!
With fun in their hearts and a twinkle in eye,
Come wear your own stories, let laughter fly!

Ever-Changing Charms

In morning light, my charms do shift,
A rabbit, a donut, who could resist?
With every day's twist, a new vibe to wear,
My quirky allure is beyond compare!

I swap out my pins like they're socks on a spree,
There's no end to the fun; it's just little me!
With humor in hand and wit on my sleeve,
Each accessory tells you, 'You can believe!'

Lunch with the crew, oh what should I choose?
A taco-shaped pin or a tiny red shoe?
The laughter erupts, 'It's such a delight!'
"Oh, look at her charm!" they squeal in the night.

No season too dull for my sparkling flair,
With every new outfit, a story to share.
The charms keep on changing, with each fun design,
A mirror of whimsy, forever divine!

The Allure of Adornment

Oh, the thrill of a pendant that dances and sways,
With a wink from my earrings, life's better in ways.
My collection is wild, a delightful parade,
Each piece holds a secret, a story well-played.

Costumes of laughter, oh, what a mix!
With gems from the thrift shop to make people tick!
A pizza slice dangling, or an avocado?
It's the allure of adornment; come join the show!

At silly brunches, I upcycle my threads,
Eating confetti, with laughter that spreads.
From kitten motif hats to a daisy brooch,
In the garden of fun, we'll happily roach.

So here's to the glamour that tickles our bones,
With joy in the tiny things, let laughter be known!
In vibrant array, we embrace every hue,
Life's too short for dullness, let's sparkle anew!

The Versatile Pin

On my lapel, a tiny friend,
It sparkles bright, no need to blend.
A unicorn today, a fish tomorrow,
What a joy, what a laugh, no room for sorrow.

It's a winter snowman, adorned with flair,
Come summer, it's a sun, with rays to share.
With hearts in spring, all colors fair,
I wear my moods like hats to wear.

Sometimes it's quirky, a silly cat,
Or a slice of pizza, where's my hat?
Forget my outfit, it's the pin that wins,
Throw on some laughter as the day begins!

So when you see me with my little gem,
Just know it's fun, and not a big hem.
Fashion rules? Nah, let's bend and play,
With my versatile pin, it's a funny parade!

Cascade of Colors

In spring's bouquet, I find my muse,
A cluster of colors, I gladly choose.
A splash of orange, a hint of blue,
Wearing my garden, oh, how it grew!

Summer days bring a wild array,
Frilly florals blooming, come what may.
A polka-dot pin with a wink and grin,
It's a riot of colors, let's begin!

Autumn arrives, foliage so bright,
I sport a pin shaped like pumpkin delight.
Leaves dance around, in a swirling spree,
Who knew my wardrobe would be so free?

Winter months chill, but my heart's aglow,
I stick on a snowflake, watch it flow.
Cascade of colors, a laughter storm,
In this wild fashion, we all transform!

Seasons in Bloom

Spring brings blossoms, a daisy charm,
A tiny pin where flowers swarm.
Rolling in colors, giggles too,
It's a lively dance, oh yes, woohoo!

Flip to summer, my map is set,
A watermelon slice, surprised? Not yet!
My lapel's a buffet, come take a taste,
Each day's an adventure, none goes to waste.

Then comes autumn, let's have some fun,
A leaf on my jacket, let's do a run!
Chasing the winds, I wear my glee,
Nature and laughter, it's wild and free!

Winter's magic, a snowman's pride,
With a scarf and a laugh, I take a ride.
Seasons in bloom, with wit to share,
Fashion's a comedy, join if you dare!

Ties of Time and Trend

With a knot and a twist, oh what a sight,
A classic pin brings the past to light.
Old-school vibes with a modern flair,
Ties of time, we're beyond compare!

Forget the fads, let's create a scene,
With vintage buttons and fabrics unseen.
It's a retro party on my fancy coat,
Wearing the past with a giggling note!

Catch me in plaid or polka dots bright,
Dressed up for fun, oh what a delight!
Each pin tells a story, I'm quite the trend,
With a chuckle and a wink, let's not pretend!

So here's to fashion that never gets old,
With humor and charm, and stories bold.
Ties of time and trend, let laughter reign,
Dancing through life, we'll never feel plain!

Seasons Wrapped in Elegance

In springtime's bloom, a flashy pin,
It dances light with a cheeky grin.
Yellow petals twist and sway,
"Wear me, darling!" they seem to say.

Summer's heat brings a fruity flair,
A slice of lemon, with style to spare.
"Sizzle and shine!" it flashes bright,
In the sun, it's pure delight.

Autumn leaves in hues of rust,
A cozy pin draped with trust.
"Crunch the leaves, come twirl with me!"
Falling style, so wild and free.

Winter chill wraps a frosty gem,
"I keep your heart warm!" it shouts, ahem.
A snowflake pin with quirks galore,
Add some laughter, who could ask for more?

Glimmers of Change

A pin that changes with each new day,
It sparkles louder than what words say.
Worn on a whim for laughs and fun,
In every season, it's never done.

Spring twists in shades of bright delight,
With bunnies and flowers, it takes flight.
Chasing clouds and weather whims,
Dancing to nature's whimsical hymns.

Summer arrives, feels like a tease,
With ice cream cones and a light breeze.
A bright sunburst shimmering plays,
On long, lazy, sun-filled days.

Autumn brings hints of spooky cheer,
A pumpkin pin makes everyone near.
"Boo!" it giggles with a wink,
In the fall, let's laugh and think.

Winter's chill is a frosty dream,
A snowman pin brings you to scream.
It wobbles and jiggles, oh what a sight,
Keeping spirits warm through the night.

Crafted Whispers

A daisy blooms, adorned with flair,
It winks and whispers, "I'm fun to wear!"
Each gentle laugh, each sunny jest,
Adorning your heart, never a test.

Bumblebees buzz, a comic chase,
A pin that paints a smile on your face.
"Catch me if you can!" it uses charm,
With laughter, joy, it floods the farm.

Winter greets with knitted care,
A cozy gem, perfect to wear.
"Snug as a bug, in a warm scarf!"
A whimsical scene that makes you laugh.

Each season wraps a tale so bright,
With pins that twinkle day and night.
To wear your laughter, let it shine,
A crafted secret, a pin divine.

The Harmony of Time

Tick tock, each season spins,
A jeweled tock that invites grins.
Spring sings sweet with blooms in play,
Each pin a note in life's ballet.

Summer laughs with a bright sun pin,
"Join the beach party, let's begin!"
Waves of fun crash on the shore,
Where giggles and splashes offer more.

Autumn whispers with crunchy sound,
A leaf-shaped pin that spins around.
"Catch my colors, feel the breeze!"
Dancing in swirls among the trees.

Winter glows with a frosty shimmer,
"I'll keep you warm, your smile's a winner!"
With each twinkle of a jeweled star,
A cozy pin, close and far.